The Ayurveda

GW00786726

<u>Ayurveda</u>

Ayurvedic Healing For Health, Yoga And Weight Loss, Mindful Eating, Anti Aging And More!

Sarah Brooks

STOP!!! Before you read any further….Would you like to know the secrets of becoming a meditation expert?

If your answer is YES, YES PICK ME you are not alone. Thousands of people are learning the incredible benefits of meditation and how it can help you gain control in your mental and physical life.

If you have been searching for these answers for gaining better understanding about meditation and the secrets to mastering this skill, you have stumbled upon the right place!

Not only will you gain incredible insight in this book, but because I want to make sure to give you as much value as possible, right now you can get full **100% FREE access to a VIP bonus Ebook** on the **Secrets of Becoming A Meditation Expert in 7 Days or Less!**

<u>**Just Go Here For Free Instant Access:**</u>

<u>www.MeditateMind.com</u>

Legal Notice

Disclaimer Notice

they see applicable.

Table Of Contents

Introduction

I want to thank you and congratulate you for purchasing the book, *"The Ayurveda Ultimate Guide! Ayurveda: Ayurvedic Healing For Health, Yoga And Weight Loss, Mindful Eating, Anti Aging And More!"*

This book contains proven steps and strategies on how to practice Ayurveda. This is a very ancient healing system, originating from the ancient Indian civilization. It has been practiced for thousands of years and has been proven to provide various health benefits.

Learn what Ayurveda is all about. In this book, you will get to know what Ayurveda specifically does in order to promote health. This practice not only keeps the body healthy, but also the mind and the spirit.

Read on and find out more about Ayurveda. Also, learn how you can achieve overall health, weight loss, and living a healthy and happy life.

Thanks again for purchasing this book, I hope you enjoy it!

Chapter 1: Understanding Ayurveda

Ayurveda is an ancient traditional healing practice. It uses the holistic or "whole body" healing system. The practice originated from the ancient Indian civilization.

The practice stems from the belief that health is achieved through maintaining harmony between the body, spirit, and mind. Creating and maintaining the balance is a delicate process that determines wellness and health.

Concepts in Ayurveda

Ayurveda revolves around the theory that everything that exists in the universe is connected to each other. Existence is in harmony with the rest of the universe.

Within the body, this same harmony should also exist in order to achieve good health. There should be harmony between the mind and body, as well as the spirit. These 3 elements should also be in harmony with the rest of the universe. Disruption in the balance causes sickness and poor health.

Ayurveda is firmly based on the concept that the spirit, body and mind are all connected. Maintaining the balance is the most important focus of Ayurveda. The basic tenets of Ayurveda based on this central concept are:

- All things are connected, whether living or nonliving things. Each thing contains the same basic 5 elements of earth, air, water, space, and fire.

- The body and the environment have a deep connection.

- There is a connection from the body, to the people around it, to its immediate environment, and to the rest of the universe. Balance among these supports good health.

- Health is retained if the balance is maintained, through wholesome, effective interaction with the environment.

- The initial balance is often disrupted by the lifestyle one leads. Choices in profession, relationships, diet, and exercise creates imbalances in the physical, spiritual, and emotional aspects.

- Imbalance disrupts harmony and invites diseases.

- Restoring and maintaining balance is a conscious act. Each person has the responsibility to take steps in achieving harmony within the self and with the environment.

Anything can disrupt the balance by affecting the emotional, physical and spiritual well-being. Some of those that can cause disruption include:

- injuries
- emotional stress
- genetic or birth defects
- age
- climate and seasonal changes

In Ayurveda, people have the 5 basic elements of the universe within them. These are:

- space: related to expansiveness
- fire: related to heat, fire and transformation
- air: related to mobility, lack of form and gaseousness
- earth: related to stability and solidity
- water: related to instability and liquidity

In the body, these elements combine to form the doshas, the life energies or forces. These doshas work together and control how the body functions. There are 3 doshas working in the body, namely:

- vata dosha (combination of the element of air and space)
- kapha dosha (earth and water)
- pitta dosha (water and fire)

The Doshas

The doshas are inherited. The mix of doshas in each person is unique. Most often, one dosha appears to be more dominant over the others. Each of the doshas has specific body functions to control. Imbalance in the doshas and in their functions is held in Ayurveda as one of the factors that determine sickness and health.

Vata dosha

Vata dosha is the combination of air and space. This is considered in Ayurveda as the most powerful of the three doshas. The vata dosha controls the basic body functions like cellular division. Vata dosha is considered as the moving force behind the kapha dosha and the pitta dosha. The center of this energy is in the colon. It balances emotion and thoughts. It also supports activity, clear comprehension, and creativity.

A person with a dominant vata dosha tends to be restless, alert, and quick. They are also fearful, anxious and nervous. These people are at higher risk for the following health problems:

- constipation
- arthritis
- flatulence
- insomnia
- nerve disorders

Balancing vata includes avoidance of extreme temperatures, maintaining calm and routine, and getting adequate rest. The energy of vata increases as one ages.

Vata controls the following functions:

- breathing
- mind
- heart function
- blood flow
- excretion via the intestines

There are things that can affect the vata dosha and disrupt its normal function, such as the following:

- grief
- fear
- eating dry fruit
- staying up late
- inadequate time in between meals

Disruptions in the vata dosha can increase the risk of developing the following health problems:

- anxious feelings
- asthma attacks
- cardiovascular disease
- disorders of the nervous system
- rheumatoid arthritis
- skin irritations

Pitta dosha

The pitta dosha is a combination of the elements of water and fire. Pitta dosha regulates the chemical, digestive, and metabolic functions. It is often associated with oiliness and heat. The center of this energy is the small intestines.

Energy from the pitta dosha adds a healthy glow to the skin, eyes, and hair. It controls the following bodily functions:

- digestion
- metabolic processes to break down ingested foods

- hormones that control appetite

Dominance of this dosha supports a hearty appetite and efficient metabolism. People with this dosha dominance tend to be aggressive and intelligent achievers.

In terms of health, the dominance of pitta dosha makes a person prone to the following health problems:

- nausea and vomiting
- inflammatory conditions
- rashes
- diarrhea
- bleeding disorders
- anger

Balance is achieved by avoiding exposure to extreme heat and limiting eating spicy food.

The pitta dosha can be disrupted by the following:

- fatigue
- eating foods that are spicy
- eating foods that are sour
- too much exposure to the sun

Disruptions in the pitta dosha increase the risk for the development of the following health problems:

- heart disease
- high blood pressure
- anger
- negative emotions
- infections
- Crohn's disease
- heartburn (often a few hours after eating)

Kapha dosha

This dosha is composed of the elements of earth and water. It controls the following bodily functions:

- growth of muscles
- weight
- stability and strength
- immune system

Factors that can disrupt the kapha dosha include the following:

- sleeping during the day
- greed
- eating even after the stomach is already full
- eating lots of sweet foods
- too much intake of salt or water

Imbalance in the kapha dosha increases the chances of a person suffering from the following:

- asthma and other respiratory disorders
- diabetes
- cancer
- obesity
- nausea, often experienced a few minutes after eating

The seat or center of kapha is in the stomach. It is related to all things that involve mucus and lubrication. It is also related to the arterial system as well as the immune system.

According to Ayurveda, the kapha dosha produces energy that promotes healing and self-repair. It allows for endurance. Energy from kapha dosha provides psychological and physical stability and strength. In terms of emotions, it promotes patience, understanding, empathy, forgiveness, compassion, love and loyalty.

People with dominant kapha have strong personalities. They are loving and are known to be tolerant. They are also tenacious, but can keep calm at the same time.

In as far as health is concerned, the dominance of kapha energy makes a person naturally prone to the following problems:

- lethargy
- weight gain
- goiter
- excessive sleep
- pulmonary congestion
- asthma
- allergies

Health maintenance is achieved through regular exercise, avoidance of napping, and eating light meals.

Chapter 2: Health Through Ayurvedic Healing

Ayurveda is concerned more about promoting health, rather than about curing ailments. Treatments target restoring balance within the body, in relation to the energies and elements of the universe. It depends on the primary dosha, the praktiri and the overall balance of the elements.

Panchakarma

Treatment is focused on cleansing the body by getting rid of undigested food. This is called the ama, which tends to stick to the body tissues and cause sickness. The process of cleansing is called panchakarma, which aims to reduce symptoms and to return the balance and harmony in the body. The goals of panchakarma include:

- restoring balance
- reducing symptoms
- improving spiritual healing
- boosting the immunity

The treatment process of panchakarma includes the following activities:

- massage
- blood purification, through special teas or blood letting
- emesis (induced vomiting)
- medical oils administered through the nose
- use of laxatives, enemas, or purgatives (to cleanse the intestines)

Other treatments that may be done in panchakarma, depending on several factors include:

- aromatherapy
- changes in the diet
- breathing exercises
- spices and plant-based oils
- administration of vitamins, herbs, minerals, and metals
- changes in unhealthy lifestyle
- stretching
- meditation
- yoga

Chapter 3: Yoga For Health

Yoga is integral to the practice of Ayurveda. They are interrelated branches of the entire concept of the Vedas. They are separate disciplines, but are interrelated. Their concepts and practices often overlap, too.

Yoga is part of the Vedic philosophy. In fact, it is one of the philosophy's 6 systems. It is the system of *sadhana* or spiritual practice. While it is a separate system, yoga actually encompasses all the other systems. It is a representation of the practical side of these other systems. Yoga also outlines the major principles and methods needed in order to develop a meditative mind, which is Vedic knowledge's basis.

Yoga is not originally meant as a healing system. It was a pursuit to spiritual health. The practice does not intend to treat psychological or physical ailments. The goal of yoga is to relieve spiritual suffering, which is totally useful in Ayurveda. Remember that Ayurveda aims to balance the mind, the spirit, and the body. The spirit part is taken care of by yoga practice.

Yoga is not originally for medical purposes. But it can be turned towards the direction of healing, towards that of Ayurveda.

Yoga Therapy

The yoga approach to health integrates the Ayurvedic principles of harmonizing the mind, spirit, and body. It unites, integrates, combines and creates harmony among the senses, consciousness, prana, mind, and body.

Real yoga therapy is different from simply following certain postures. It is not merely the physical practice. In order to achieve health, consider all the 8 limbs of yoga. The 1st 2 of the 8 limbs are yamas and niyamas. These refer to the yogic practices and principles of right living. The yamas and niyamas are the foundations that can sustain healing practice and spiritual health.

Asana

The asana is only the external medical portion of the practice of yoga. It is used to treat disorders that involve musculo-skeletal system. It can also provide other benefits indirectly. This practice can only give its healing benefits if proper diet is integrated into the practice. The body will always reflect the kind of nutrition that it receives. Poor nutrition would result in poor body function and movement. The benefits of asana are only fully appreciated when practiced within the context of lifestyle and dictary recommendations of Ayurveda.

The healing effects of asana on the body and mind are indirect. The effects are most often secondary.

Pranayama

The internal healing portion of yoga is called the pranayama. This practice restores the vital energy (prana) in the body. Pranayama helps direct the prana in several ways, depending on the body's needs. It also influences the doshas in the body.

Pranayama is effective in treating health conditions that involve the circulatory, nervous and respiratory systems. Aside from its direct healing properties on these systems, pranayama can also affect all other conditions in the body, both physical and psychological.

Manipulating the prana is integral to healing. Altering its movement and increasing its healing powers are all controlled by pranayama.

Pratyahara

Pratyahara is another important concept in yoga. Energy is internalized, which is a necessary step to achieving deep healing. It is also important in order for meditation to occur. Reaching the stage of pratyahara is necessary in order for real healing using yoga to occur.

The mind and the body must be in a relaxed state. The energy is then directed from within. This is done in various ways including massage in order for healing to start. Stimulating the pratyahara places the person in deep rest, which then allows the removal of all the toxins from the body.

Chapter 4: Meditation For Health

Meditation supports the goal of Ayurveda in restoring and maintaining balance between the mind, body and spirit. This practice takes care of the mind. The type of meditation depends on the individual dosha. For instance, a person who is kapha-dominant needs the mind to be kept busy. Someone whose mind is vata needs to kept still and quiet. A mind with pitta dosha should be relaxed and calmed. The type of meditation is also dependent on the state of tamas, sattva, or rajas.

A person with rajas and vata dosha (energy) tend to be in constant movement and irregularity. Meditation should aid in achieving stillness. Pranayama is best at restoring the balance of the vata mind and rajas state. For best results, practice meditation every day. Add a round of breathing to pranayama each day for 1 month.

Kapha-dominant minds are generally slow. The meditation practice should aim to keep the mind busy and engaged. Examples would be walking meditation, guided visualization, tai chi, and contemplative questions.

Minds dominated by pitta need to be calmed, as it is often agitated or heated. Pranayama is best for this goal. Practice breathing alternately through the nostril and through a curled tongue (called Shitali pranayama).

The type of meditation practice should address the specific individual composition of elements. When using mantra meditation, the kind of mantra used should also be well adapted to specific individuals. For example, choose mantras that can pacify the pitta. There are also mantras that can increase goodness and purity.

Chapter 5: Weight Loss With Ayurveda

The goal of Ayurveda is to promote harmony and balance within the self and with the universe. Creating this balance can also bring about weight loss. There is no need for chemicals and extreme diets in order to achieve the best weight.

8 Ayurvedic Practices for Weight Loss

Follow these practices based on Ayurvedic principles:

1. Boost the bowel function upon waking in the morning. Take a large glass of warm water mixed with freshly squeezed juice of organic lemon.

2. Engage in daily exercise, about 45 to 60 minutes in the morning to boost metabolism.

3. Meditate early in the morning for at least 5 to 10 minutes. This will prepare the mind and the body for the day's activities. It also reduces stress, which can cause weight gain.

4. Eat at regular hours, 3 meals a day. Do not have snacks. Eat a moderate breakfast anytime between 7:30 AM to 9 AM. Lunch is the heaviest meal of the day taken between 11 AM and 2 PM. Dinner is the smallest meal of the day, taken between the hours of 5:30 PM and 8 PM.

5. Eat in accordance with the prevailing season. Eat fresh vegetables and fruits that are high carbohydrate. These are

most abundant during this time. These foods will keep the body cool and provide the much needed energy. During the fall and winter seasons, abundant foods that should be eaten are stored grains, fruits, seeds, and nuts. There is also abundance in root vegetables, cheeses, and heavier meats. In the spring, cleanse the body from the acidic and heavy winter diet with sprouts, green leafy vegetables and berries.

6. Prepare a balanced diet by incorporating the 6 Ayurvedic tastes of salty, sweet, bitter, pungent, sour and astringent. Having all these in each meal assures that all the major food groups, and their nutrients are present.

   Sour, salty, and sweet tastes are considered as building foods. Excess intake can cause weight gain. Balance them with bitter, astringent and pungent tastes that are considered catabolic. Bitter foods are leafy vegetables. Astringent foods include pomegranate seeds. Pungent foods include chili peppers.

   One would notice that meals are more satisfying when all the 6 Ayurvedic tastes are present. Urges to overeat and to snack are also diminished.

7. After eating, get moving. This will stimulate digestion and peristaltic movement of the intestines. Walk for about 10-20 minutes. Lying on the left side after exercising would further improve digestion.

8. Get enough sleep. Ayurveda recommends going to bed when the sun goes down and wake up when the sun goes up. This is the natural circadian rhythm of the body. When

the body follows this natural rhythm, it creates a profound hormone balancing consequence.

When the body gets enough sleep, the body can reset and detoxify. It also reduces the levels of the hormone cortisol, which plays a major role in weight gain and obesity.

Digestive power

Good health, in Ayurveda, means the ability to metabolize the sensory, emotional, and nutritional information that a person takes in. The agni or fire is the body's digestive energy.

How to strengthen the digestive fire

In order to strengthen and improve the function of the body's digestive fire, follow these practices according to Ayurvedic principles:

- When eating, always sit down. Avoid eating while watching TV or driving. Also, avoid eating while in front of a computer.
- Eat in a calm and relaxed atmosphere. Avoid eating when upset.
- Eat only when absolutely hungry.
- Eat at a moderate pace. Avoid gulping food down, chewing food too fast or too slow.
- Limit eating raw foods because these are more difficult to digest than cooked food.
- Incorporate all of the six Ayurvedic tastes in each meal.
- Drink tea of hot water with ginger all throughout the day.
- Practice any type of moderate exercise regularly.

- Massage with herbalized oil on a daily basis to balance the mind-body.
- Meditate every day.
- Use detoxifying herbs in food. These include ashwagandha, triphala, guggulu, ginger, brahmi, neem and turmeric.

Chapter 6: Ayurvedic Mindful Eating Practices

Mindful eating means being aware of what one eats. It means being more conscious of the sensation one gets while eating, such as the taste of the food, textures, and colors. It also means being more aware of how food affects the body and how the body reacts to food. Mindful eating helps in restoring the body in relation to its balance with the mind and the spirit.

8 Principles of Ayurvedic Mindful Eating

1. Check hunger before eating.

    Make sure that one is really hungry before eating. Sometimes, cravings, emotions, and stress are disguised as feeling hungry. Close the eyes and be aware of the body. Focus the mind on the hunger and continuously evaluate hunger levels while eating.

2. Eat meals in a quiet and settled environment.

    Remove all distractions during meal times. Avoid laptops, TVs, phones, and other stimulus while eating. Digestion does not work properly when the mind is distracted.

3. Eat at a moderate pace.

    Appreciate the food. Chew the food well. Put down the spoon or fork in between mouthfuls to prevent shoveling food into the mouth.

4. Avoid eating when upset.

Emotional agitation upsets the digestive process. One will not be able to get the full benefits from the nutrients in food when eating while upset.

5. Sip small amounts of water when eating. Refrain from drinking ice cold water.

   Drinking large amounts of water can weaken the stomach's hydrochloric acid and delay digestion. Ice cold water also weakens the digestive enzymes, dampening the digestive fire.

6. The main meal should be lunch.

   The digestive fire is strongest when the sun is also at its strongest, which is in the middle of the day. This way, one can digest and metabolize food better during this time. Maximize the time and eat the most during lunch time.

7. Enjoy the food by using the senses.

   Eating is not just about the taste and smell of food. It is also about textures and color. Eat a colorful diet to stimulate sight. Food looks more appetizing when the eyes are pleased. Eat a variety of foods that have different textures, such as rough, smooth, soft, crunchy, etc.

8. Sit after eating.

   Enjoy eating further by giving the body a chance to savor the meal after it is finished. Sit back for 5 minutes. This will allow the body to fully wallow in the satisfaction of eating. It also aids the digestive process by giving it a chance to act on the food. Digestion happens best when the body is at rest.

Chapter 7: Ayurvedic Superfoods

According to the principles of Ayurveda, food is changed into life force energy that is vital to the body. Eating aims to support inner strength and to boost immunity. It also helps to clear the mind, improve circulation, and support a more powerful digestion.

Superfoods in Ayurveda are simple, everyday foods that are super-charged to improve health. These foods affect the balance within the body and with the rest of the universe. Eating the right kinds of foods can help prevent fatigue and illness.

Astralagus root

This is a powerful adaptogen. It helps the body resist the negative effects of illness and stress. It helps the body restore its normal function. Astralagus root can be added to broths, stews, pots of grains and soups.

Whole Coriander Seed and Black Pepper

These are among the most beneficial spices. They are great at detoxifying the body. Coriander seeds are considered in Ayurveda as a spice that regulates digestion. A good digestion supports a strong immune system. Black pepper is a spice good for promoting healthy circulation. Add these 2 spices together in a pepper grinder and use about ¼ teaspoon to every meal.

Garlic

The most benefits are obtained from raw garlic. It works great during the cold and damp weathers. It helps fight colds and flu, as well as other infections. It is good to consume garlic during the winter season to strengthen the body. Add raw garlic to soups, teas and broth.

Turmeric

Turmeric has very potent antioxidant and anti-inflammatory properties. It helps the body digest proteins. The pungent, astringent, and bitter tastes are great in balancing the body during the winter.

Ginger

This is considered as the universal medicine in Ayurveda. It has healing, anti-inflammatory, energizing, expectorating, and warming effects. It is also a stimulating spice. Ginger encourages a healthy appetite. It also calms indigestion. Ginger is also great at supporting good circulation within the body.

Foods rich in Vitamin C

The list includes oranges, lemons, grapefruit, broccoli, and Brussels sprouts. Other less popular, but equally super charged with vitamin C are fresh raspberries, acerola berries and strawberries. Amla berries are known to contain one of the highest vitamin C concentrations in natural whole foods.

Vitamin C boosts the immunity. It is especially needed during the winter. Foods rich in vitamin C are light, warm, and promote circulation. Vitamin C acts as an antioxidant that supports immunity, healthy tissue growth and collagen production. Get at least 300 mg of vitamin C a day. In times of infection, aim to have more.

Ghee

This is clarified butter, which means buttermilk and milk solids are removed. Ghee is easily digested. It rekindles the agni and supports the sattvic and ojas in the body.

Basmati rice

This is easy to digest. People with weak agni can still easily digest Basmati rice. The grains are long, with a delicate flavor and smell.

Saffron

This is one of the most valued exotic spices. It increases the effects of foods taken with it. It is considered a sattvic food. It has potent healing properties on the heart, blood and reproductive system. Saffron is best eaten after it is soaked in warm milk.

Chapter 8: Ayurvedic Natural Remedies & Healing Foods

Aside from foods that provide nourishment and strengthen bodily functions, there are foods that can be used to target certain illnesses. These healing foods can be used as natural remedies to some illnesses, without having to use chemical drugs.

Lemons

These are natural detoxifiers that cleanse the body. By getting rid of toxins, the body is able to function better and heal faster. Recovering from stress and illnesses occur much faster after the body is detoxified.

Figs and Dates

These are great in boosting the body's energy levels. These also help in building tissues.

Mung beans

These are highly recommended for people suffering from various sicknesses. Mung beans are easily digested and boost the overall health.

Cumin seeds

These are great at aiding the digestive process. It also helps in removing toxins from the body.

Natural Remedies

- For toothaches, Ayurvedic practice recommends chewing on a clove of garlic.

- For difficulty falling asleep, mix 1 cup of warm milk with a pinch of cinnamon and 4-5 pieces of dates. Drink at bedtime.

- For a restful sleep, massage the soles of the feet and the palms with warm oil like sesame oil.

- For cough, mix ginger juice and honey. Ginger is an expectorant that draws mucus out. Honey soothes throat irritated from all the coughing.

Chapter 9: Anti-Aging Benefits Of Ayurveda

Anti-aging effects and maintaining youthful beauty are also promoted by the practices of Ayurveda. Here are the 9 Ayurvedic anti-aging properties being practiced and found effective.

Vayasthapana

It means "stopping age" or "maintaining youthfulness." The gotu kola is a popular herb used in Ayurveda for its anti-aging effect. It supports collagen synthesis for better skin quality.

Varnya

This means enhancing the bright complexion of the skin, making it more radiant. Herbs that promote varnya include rose petals, costus, Indian redwood and silk cotton tree.

Sandhanya

This involves protecting the skin from the daily, normal wear and tear. The herbs of sandhanya promote both skin regenerative and healing functions. It also promotes the repair of skin damaged because of the aging effects of normal daily life. An example is the sensitive plant, which promotes sandhanya.

Branropana

This means deep healing. The herbs promote the skin's ability for deeper healing. Gotu kola and sensitive plant are examples of herbs that promote branropana. They are best known for promoting wound healing,

Twachya

This means enhancing and nurturing the skin. The herbs of twachya provide an overall nourishment and moisture balance to the skin. Examples are gotu kola, rose petals, and silk cotton tree.

Shothahara

This refers to the anti-inflammatory effects on the skin. The herbs protect the skin from inflammatory substances, allergens, stress and chemicals that can cause skin aging. Examples are aloe vera, rose petals, silk cotton tree and costus.

Twachagnivardhani

This involves the strengthening the skin's metabolism. It enhances the heath and luster of the skin by strengthening the metabolic processes within the skin cells. As one ages, metabolism slows and cause buildup of toxins and other impurities. This cases skin dryness, dullness and wrinkles. To prevent this, boost the cellular metabolism to get rid of all the toxins that case aging. An example is gotu kola.

Twagrasayana

This is the process of retarding skin aging by maintaining the health of the skin. The herbs promote well-being and longevity.

Chapter 10: Ayurvedic Approach To Feeling Good

Ayurveda aims to maintain health by preventing illness. Curing illnesses is only secondary to the practices of Ayurveda. In order to maintain health, Ayurveda recommends following a daily and seasonal regimen that creates balance between the self and the environment. This is based on the concept that health is related to the harmonious relationship of the self with diet, seasonal changes, day and night, lifestyle choices, and other internal and external factors.

Understanding the body's constitution (prana, dosha, etc)

The first step to feeling good, living healthy and healing the body is by understanding the unique body-mind type of a person. Find out what dosha is dominant. Determining these factors helps in determining what unique and specific needs to address. It helps in making the best choices about exercises, diet, and supplements to incorporate in life.

Diet of colorful and flavorful foods

Eating is one of the most vital functions in the body. Food should be nourishing in order to achieve a healthy mind and body. To obtain the best nutrition, eat a variety of foods that are fresh and organic. Full awareness should be exercised when preparing and eating food.

Aside from the 6 tastes, meals should also include variety of colors. Food looks more appetizing this way. It also promotes a healthy long life. One can also literally eat the energies of the universe through the colorful foods.

Colorful foods also contain important compounds that boost the immunity. They contain antioxidants that strengthen against illnesses and enhance the body's health. Include colors like orange, red, purple, green and deep blue.

Enough restful sleep

Sleep is considered as the nursemaid to humans, according to Ayurveda. The body gets the chance to repair itself. It is also the time for the body to rejuvenate. When a person does not get enough sleep, the internal balance is disrupted. The immune system is weakened, which increases susceptibility to illnesses and infections. It also accelerates aging.

The body needs restful sleep, about 6 to 8 hours. Sleep needs to be restful. This means natural sleep, without the aid of chemical drugs and alcohol. Restful sleep will make one feel vibrant and more energetic upon waking up. Feeling unenthusiastic and tired when one wakes up means that he did not have restful sleep during the previous night.

Becoming attuned to nature

Living in tune with nature means gaining healthy desires that can very well provide what one needs. According to Ayurveda, nature made humans, therefore, their needs and wants should be in tune with the elements and balance of nature.

The presence of balance creates a natural desire geared towards nurturing life and health. There is a harmonious flow of the body's rhythm and functions. Slipping out of tune with nature creates unnatural desires that are not geared towards nurturing. There are unhealthy cravings and compulsive behaviors such as craving junk foods and neglecting sleep and exercise. These would cause imbalance that worsens over time. This will increase the risk for health problems.

Learn to listen to the body's messages

The body knows what is best for itself. It expresses its "opinions" on things done to it by using signals of discomfort and comfort. When the body thinks that something will be good for its survival and function, it sends a signal of eagerness and comfort. If something threatens the integrity of the body, it sends signals of emotional and physical distress. Learn to listen to what the body is trying to say and make decisions based on these.

According to Ayurveda, the body lives in the now. It never harbors any doubts about itself. The body is intrinsically wired to preserve itself and listening to it means following the instinct to nurture and survive.

Conclusion

Thank you again for purchasing this book on *The Ayurveda Ultimate Guide! Ayurveda: Ayurvedic Healing For Health, Yoga And Weight Loss, Mindful Eating, Anti Aging And More!*

I am extremely excited to pass this information along to you, and I am so happy that you now have read and can hopefully implement these strategies going forward.

I hope this book was able to help you understand what Ayurveda is all about and how to use the practices and concepts to achieve a healthier you.

The next step is to get started using this information and to hopefully live a better, healthier and balanced life! Harness natural energies to enjoy your life to the fullest with ayurvedic healing practices.

Please don't be someone who just reads this information and doesn't apply it, the strategies in this book will only benefit you if you use them!

If you know of anyone else that could benefit from the information presented here please inform them of this book.

Finally, if you enjoyed this book and feel it has added value to your life in any way, please take the time to share your thoughts and post a review on Amazon. It'd be greatly appreciated!

Thank you and good luck!

Preview Of:

Ultimate Coconut Oil Guide!

<u>Coconut Oil</u>

Coconut Oil Recipes For Organic Skin Care And Natural Beauty, Clean Eating For Weight Loss, Shinning Hair, Better Brain Function And Overall Health!

Introduction

I want to thank you and congratulate you for purchasing the book, *Coconut Oil: Ultimate Coconut Oil Guide! - Coconut Oil Recipes For Organic Skin Care And Natural Beauty, Clean Eating For Weight Loss, Shining Hair, Better Brain Function And Overall Health!*

This book contains proven steps and strategies on how you can take full advantage of the beauty, weight loss and health benefits that coconut oil has to offer. Through this book, you will learn more about:

- What makes coconut oil healthy?

- How it can help you get better, more glowing skin.

- Its effects on your hair and making healthier.

- Can coconut oil improve your brain function?

- Weight loss benefits and how it can boost your metabolism.

- Coconut oil and how it can help treat different illnesses.

- Recipes for both your diet as well as organic skin care.

- How to choose the right coconut oil for your needs.

We hope that through this book, you'll be able to recognize the amount of potential that a single bottle of coconut oil contains.

Thanks again for purchasing this book, I hope you enjoy it!

Chapter 1: Coconut Oil For Natural Beauty And Health

These days, more and more people are becoming aware of the effects that chemically manufactured products has on their bodies. As such, many of them have turned to a greener, more organic lifestyle that advocates going all natural when it comes to their food as well as the different products that they use on their bodies.

This isn't surprising, of course, considering the fact that there are a number of illnesses which are associated with constant use of synthetic and often chemical-laden skin and health products. There are certain risks that one must bear when using it; risks which can be avoided altogether if one were to switch over to something that's a bit closer to nature.

The coconut oil is a favorite among health buffs as it is one of those by-products that can be used in a multitude of ways. On one hand, it can be eaten and taken as a supplement which would boost your overall health. On the other, it can be applied topically and used as a beauty product as well as a means of treating certain skin issues.

You get all of these benefits but without worrying about its harmful effects to the body.

Why is it considered one of the best natural remedies out there?

It's all in the composition. About 99% of it is composed of saturated fats (which, in this case isn't as bad as it sounds) as well as traces of polyunsaturated fatty acids and monosaturated fatty acids. Virgin coconut oil retains a higher amount of the good stuff thus it is also valued higher.

It also contains lauric acid and quite a generous amount of it at that. When digested by the body, this would turn into monolaurin and is very beneficial when it comes to dealing with different bacteria and viruses. Diseases such as influenza and herpes are just two of the things that coconut oil can cure in a jiff. A tablespoon of it a day keeps the doctor away, so to speak.

Besides these, it is also one of the most powerful inhibitors of quite a number of different pathogenic organisms ranging from your usual viruses to even protozoa. All of this, of course, is attributed to its high lauric acid content.

For beauty and skincare

Coconut can also be used for cosmetic or skin care purposes. We'll get to the specifics of this in later chapters but to quickly summarize, it is often used for: Hair care, skin care, nails, lips as well as treating different skin issues such as psoriasis. It helps keep the skin youthful and glowing as well as protect it from harmful UV rays.

Thanks for Previewing My Exciting Book Entitled:

"Coconut Oil: Ultimate Coconut Oil Guide! Coconut Oil Recipes For Organic Skin Care And Natural Beauty, Clean Eating For Weight Loss, Shinning Hair, Better Brain Function And Overall Health!"

To purchase this book, simply go to the Amazon Kindle store and simply search:

"COCONUT OIL"

Then just scroll down until you see my book. You will know it is mine because you will see my name "Sarah Brooks" underneath the title.

Alternatively, you can visit my author page on Amazon to see this book and other work I have done. Thanks so much, and please don't forget your free bonuses

DON'T LEAVE YET! - CHECK OUT YOUR FREE BONUSES BELOW!

Free Bonus Offer: Get Free Access To The www.MeditateMind.com VIP Newsletter!

Once you enter your email address you will immediately get free access to this awesome newsletter!

But wait, right now if you join now for free you will also get free access the "Secrets of Becoming A Meditation Expert – In 7 Days!" free Ebook!

To claim both your FREE VIP NEWSLETTER MEMBERSHIP and your FREE BONUS Ebook on the SECRETS OF BECOMING A MEDITATION EXPERT IN 7 DAYS!

Just Go To:

www.MeditateMind.com

20458012R00026

Printed in Great Britain
by Amazon